PRAISE FOR *WASH*

I never feel more held or challenged than when I am witnessing Ebony Stewart's poems. Her voice is unmistakable, requires you to sit up and pay attention. These poems do exactly what they promise—get right to the thick mud of it all and call forth a cleansing. By the time you finish this book, you'll be hanging loneliness out to dry (and maybe cussing a few people out who deserve it). Let *WASH* do the work it came to do, and get baptized in Ebony's queer Black womxn glory.

— Ariana Brown, author of *We Are Owed*

Courageous enough to unbury and tell the truth. Rigorously trained enough to tend to the Light while breaking us Open. Baddass enough to make us laugh a hell yesss out into the room. These poems unpack what we been carrying. This poet is a Priestess. She slays/she conjures/she fights...with every word for us all to be free. We Black womxn. We queer. We children. We grannys. We tender ones. Bless this Gully queen. And Bless yo self. Git dis book. And spread the word.

— Sharon Bridgforth, writer and USA Artist Fellow

Vulnerability and boldness do not often coexist, but Ebony Stewart braids them into every poem in *WASH*. Navigating between the emotional labor expected of Black women and the Hallelujah of the matriarchs in her lineage, Stewart carries us through a cleansing, a freeing, a search for self and the joy we house. *WASH* is the manual instructing us back into being our own version of pure, whole, powerful while telling our own stories. Ebony has given us her heart in all its raw and perfect glory.

— Yesika Salgado, author of *Corazón*

WASH

WASH

poems by:

Ebony Stewart

Button Publishing Inc.
Minneapolis
2025

WASH
POETRY
AUTHOR: Ebony Stewart
EDITED BY: Michael Whalen
COVER ART: Naledi Tshegofatso Modupi
COVER DESIGN: Coral Black
AUTHOR PHOTOGRAPHY: Harris!

◇

◇

Published by Button Poetry
Minneapolis, MN 55418 | http://www.buttonpoetry.com

Manufactured in the United States of America
PRINT ISBN: 978-1-63834-120-8
EBOOK ISBN: 978-1-63834-123-9

First printing

for the womxn who will not be loved.

—bell hooks

A BODY MOUTH MARRIAGE

an offering to self

We need a god who bleeds now
whose wounds are not the end of anything
— Ntozake Shange

I,
Womxn,
take thee body to be holy, a righteous gospel and an example of how I
choose to love thyself and
others
I will have thee naked, loose, and leaking
I will have thee stretched, scared, and struggling
I will have thee plain
with or without pain
in silence and in sweet
to have and to hold,
from this day forward
for better or worse
complicated and sure
you raggedy doubt holding womxn
you not aware of the power you possess
in pxssy and in scent
so what
of the men that have shrunk out of you and left their stench
so what of once stale and bitter
thy does not have a soul,
thy is one
a found poem
a womxnly bloomed beast
one riot fire blood-thirsting centered being
learn them by your birthright and sacrifice
you are someone terrifying and strange and beautiful
someone, not everyone, will know how to love

but *above all things*[1], I will love thyself
in the shake of a night song
in the sprawled bask of day
in sickness and in health
with the same tears down the same face
be a wealthy wet
a weightless worry
I will love thy body
I will cherish thyself
I will obey thy inherited instinct to fight back in my own way
until death do us part
in times blacker than these.
According to the god we have always been
in body and in worship
in all of my worldly goods I thee endow:
I am nothing without thyself
In the name of the Mother, and of the daughter, and the Holy Spirit.
A womxn.

---

1 after Jennifer Falú

CONTENTS

WASH

HELLO

Hello, emotional labor.
Hello, girl with ramshackle mouth and devastated heart.
Hello, voice found in the back of your mother's throat.
Hello, swallow that never does.
Hello, reaching pulling back dust.
Hello, world falling apart.
Hello, lonely.
Hello, fxckup.
Hello, hard that doesn't trust soft.
Hello, wanna be loved.
Hello, drought winter brings &
growing summer's blood.
Hello, wanna be womxn.
Hello, oceans tank &
sharks.
And, teeth.
And, shred.
And, chewed limbs.
And, Jamaican rain shadow.
And, second line.
Hello, dry fruit still bloom.
Hello, brass tongue,
a steel band.
Hello native to this body.
Wah gawan?

DIAPHRAGM

a poem for two voices

Perfect upon the eye,

I stand

5'5 slanted brown eyes, long hair, full lips that match the breasts on my

petite frame.

Pear-shaped elastic muscle

vertical to my heart hidden beneath my diaphragm.

There are secrets

buried *shhh...*

behind my stomach

watching everything that goes

in and regurgitates out.

Secrets

never say who

I

pretend to be, they just allow me

to please the eye.

Eyes with a tint of

red

roll back unconsciously, seeing every real red-

flag

issue that won't allow me to load-up my plate.

Excuses are like food for thought:

it's just a thought.

And I'm not hungry.

I mirror the wave of prom queens with stale vomit hiding under

bleach white veneers.

Saying

hello hello hello

to fickle plate holders troubled by a spoonful of rice.

There's a finger

this finger

attached to my hand

that makes me feel

that chose my mouth

like I'm always number one

to eject – rejecting self like comments:

I'm too skinny

I look fat

I hate the way my clothes fit

I wish someone would notice

me

exhausted from the battle,

dark circles circled the eyes,

perfectionist smiles

with a hint of hurt

bleeding through chapped lips,

obsessed

with numbers, crunched numbers, and bathrooms.

Me and bathrooms, particularly toilets, are always

ALWAYS

flushing to get rid of

SHXT

I'm not hungry I'm not hungry I'm not hungry

My mom says,

I *(you)*

should eat more.

That's a stupid fxcking thing to say...

that's SUCH A STUPID FXCKING THING TO SAY!

Doesn't she know if I eat, I'll get fat!?!

Big.

Heavy.

Large.

Obese.

Gross.

So, I keep holding my

breath

1 Mississippi... 2 Mississippi... 3 Mississippi...

on pages in my diary.

Written in blue ink is how many times

my dad has called me pretty without comparing me to my sister.

Right below it in restricted

red ink

listing calories consumed,

exercises to do,

and websites that assure me

that I don't have to, if I don't want to,

there's a picture of a pig

that looks just like *me!*

I know that.

So stop judging me... So stop judging me So stop judging me

because I know what you're thinking:

"that poor girl... she'd be so much prettier if she lost a few pounds."

not knowing that I've

done 250 crunches, ran 3 miles, and spent an hour on the elliptical

with only 1 stick of celery and a bottled water today,

what the fxck have you done!?

You're jealous You're jealous You're jealous

You're jealous.

You're jealous, because I know how to lose the weight and you don't!

Soon...

Soon I'll be free of the sound my throat makes and the grey on my tongue swallowing back emotions keeping self control headaches to myself, and irregular heartbeats like my weight,
waiting to fade.

You are my sunshine, my only sunshine.

You make me happy when skies are grey.

You'll never know dear, how much I love you.

Please, don't take my sunshine away.

TOMBOY

By definition: 1. Boyish girl. Unaware of her gender or roles associated with said gender.
Yes and

Beach or girl

> a shore; body of water covered by sand.
> Give a little bit, but always stay close to yourself.

2. By definition: an energetic, sometimes boisterous girl whose behavior is more typical of boys.
Yes and

Ocean or sea or womxn

> the expanse of salt water that covers most of the Earth's surface
> and surrounds its
> landmasses.
> savior, protector, self.

By definition:
Girl who is probably lesbian.
Okay and

Gulf or girl from the south

> a deep inlet of the sea almost surrounded by land, with a narrow mouth.

By definition:
Girl who does not attract boys because she be too masculine.
Yes and

> When you the strong one people don't check on you as much.
> Cause you don't get hurt.

Cause you can't get hurt.
Yes and

Harbor or girl or womxn
a body of water where ships and boats are stored or seek shelter
I don't know how to be soft without also being terrified of losing something.

By definition:
Gully or black girl that is street or hood
"Attitude. Dark skin. She probably loud."
Pops her lips, sucks her teeth, rolls her eyes, sways her hips. Who want it? Cause you can get it.
Yes and

I'll fxck you up!

3. Threat.

SUMMER

It is the year 1996.
It is summer.
It is hot.
The smell of sweat and crazy is everywhere.
It is a month after I become womxn and pomegranate silo.
Two days before I will wad another pair of beaded panties to the bottom
of the wastebasket.
Ruined.
Again.
I am all mouth, breasts, and booty.
Endangered.
Boys and men alike grab their piece when they see me.
This is not the way you were meant to be noticed.
They say things.
They stare too long; make you draw into yourself.
Forget they were born between a womxn's legs;
That I am the crown that makes them king.

It is June.
It is sticky.
It is humid.
The wind has forgotten about us.
It is the kind of day your father curses the Sun as soon as it hits his skin.
Your mother's grocery list, address book, and whole hand becomes a fan.
It is the kind of day you do not want to be punished or made to stay
outside.
Heated bodies just want to be cool.
But children only go indoors when they're thirsty.

It is the first time I will be licked.
The first time I will be groped and experience my own thieving.
The first time I will shout out of my skin.

The first time a boy will mistake my body for bed.
I remember.

He.

Is.

The first boy I will escape who wants me so bad he uses his teeth with
kiss.
The first boy I will wipe my wet face on.
The first boy I will use my knee against.

He.

Is.

The first boy I will hurt away.

It is the hardest I will ever run home.
The hardest thump my heart will ever beat.
It is the first time I will learn to shower thoughts,
to wash the fingerprints away.
To rub so hard I bout bleed.

To fester. To remember. To want to forget.
To call me fault. To know I should've known better.
To whisper apology to myself and passing womxn.
To want for the Universe to bring all my stolen pieces back to me.

Still waiting.

I have outlasted even myself.

This will happen again.

Little girl.

She.

Is.
Becoming.
Womxn.

And the summer has just begun.

A MILLION LITTLE PIECES

most days im not sure i should love you
other days
im jenga block/squared/to pieces
you dont appreciate little bitty things like tears/
especially when they happen as often as they do
i dont/wipe/anymore
youre not supposed to touch collectors items
and/fingers leave marks like ink do pages

we are gooood/at lying on our backs
and everybody knows that womxn care/
on/thick or thin sheets
i keep/leaving my heart so i can have a reason/
to go back
its clear/i should never go back
not even for my   toothbrush   panties   or hair bow
you dont appreciate little bitty things like tears/but

i wore your t-shirt to bed last night/
so i could dream about you
even there/i love you/more/than/you do/me
and i often wonder how big pain has to be/
before it stops
and so I called you/to come over
you never reject me at night/
and the only time I feel bad
is when the day catches me in bed/
by myself
but right now/we are not speaking
theres not a lot to say
and i have grown woman embarrassment/
stunting my growth

a week will go by/and/i/will do good not to call you/
or say your name
ive got to get used to thinking of myself

like the fact that i used to wash yo nasty ass drawers
or
how much flavor id put in food/
if i knew you were going to eat it
suddenly/ive forgotten what my favorites taste like
i am cereal in a bowl
i cant even make a sandwich worth eating
it hurts to chew/and swallowing this expired/love/gone bad

makes my stomach turn
and then you called me/to come over
you know i have a need to be needed
like/clocks do time
i am running out of reasons to keep my clothes on
straw/you will say/you wrote that one poem for me
camel/i will believe you between my legs
back/we are gooood/at lying on our backs

and everybody knows that womxn care/
on/thick or thin sheets
so why do i keep going back
we both know how this is going to end/
me in tears
but/you dont appreciate little bitty things/

like tears

and I gotta ask
if I were 68 shades in 50 states/
would that be enough to keep you on my lips
i am tired/of being a house call

i wanna be somewhere more permanent
i wanna be like your cell phone/
i never see you leave home without it
physically/is that not a small thing

you aint even gotta lie to me about who she is

just tell me/who tf/she is

i am easy to please
but/the one thing I need/you are unwilling to give
not even/a little/bit

DOMESTIC

For the boy on the basketball court who started a fight with my
  ex-boyfriend
and told him he hits like a girl,
to prove you wrong
he now hits girls too.

To his dad, who taught him how to kiss the girls and make
  them cry,
not only does he have your smile,
he also has your fist of rage
and unapologetic regrets.
Oh yeah,
and his left is just as strong as his right.
To his mother, who said, "sometimes women need to know when
  they are getting out of line,"
you would be proud to know that when he raises his voice
it's enough to leave a bruise.
He'll do anything to make you happy.

For his best friend, who is also his roommate, and watched me lie
  on the floor in a fetal position,
and closed the door because it wasn't his business,
and listened to my skin split between his knuckles,
congratulations on your baby girl.

To the father at the 7-Eleven who had to teach his son
that a man should never put his hands on a womxn,
I'm sorry if your son had more questions than you had answers.
Thank you for asking me twice if I was okay.
You remind me of humanity.
But if you were ready to be a hero, you'd have known I was too
  afraid to say no.

Mr. Officer,
you confirmed that I am a good actress and I must deserve
this award.
I will remember you if ever I am being too optimistic in believing
that help is on the way
and he will stop long enough for me to wipe the blood from my
bottom lip.

Poets who think I don't know how to be vulnerable, that want me
to unball my fists,
I am protecting myself.
You should've seen what happened when I didn't.

To my father, whose first time being a dad was when I called you
with the blues
and you had a lump in your throat the size of Texas.
You remember the types of beats you used to make on my
mother.
Your silence was deafening.
We be a house of blues, daddio.
Baby Girl's got heart.
She's got eyes like your favorite song.

My mother,
who knows me as her golden,
who always blended her smile and strength with blush,
I am embarrassed.
Please touch me up.
Mommy, don't ask for the details.
Do you remember when you didn't want to talk about it?
Can you just hold me
call me baby
make healing like "I love you"?
I need beautiful sounds like that.

To my ex-boyfriend,
whose touches feel like thunder,
whose words bring rain.
I still think about you in my bones
and frontal lobe
when people tell me they love me.
You win.

For anyone who has to come behind him,
I'm sorry it won't be easy.
Can you love me in a way we can both agree on?
Only use words I can recognize and please don't use mine
  against me.
There is a difference.
Pay attention to my body to know which parts are storing pain.
Memorize how many muscles it takes to smile and make sure my
  face isn't missing any.
If ever you make me cry,
be soft enough to make them stop.
You don't have to show
  how strong you are
all the time.

HONEY BADGER

The walls started to pop their own pimples and peel away from
the sheet rock, like bubble gum adhesive.
The knobs stayed in place, but there was nothing on the other
side, but a black hole where psychopaths throw away the bodies.
The carpet
stuck to the bottom of any feet, trying to get out.
Trying to escape,
its curl dried.
It smells of rot and things that cannot be repaired.
The dirt rises and tries to evaporate.
When this doesn't work, arms grow from grain and try to speak
in dust.
The windows plea.
They say things.
Anger does not see clearly.
Everything is black.
A nigger.
The tile in the kitchen becomes green slugs.
I will kill them before they get to the drain.
All the clocks have a Rolodex.
Zero
is flashing until it runs out of breath.
The stairs are trying to lose weight,
to disappear.
There is no corner that my furniture hasn't moved to.
The bathroom is praying with the closet.
Both might as well be my fist.
You forget how hard you can hit when you're trying to hurt
something.
The pages where I write my poetry have surrendered.
They will probably be there when I get out.
My brain becomes a cuff.

I have started speaking in my 'alien given voice.'
It can be scary trying to figure out what an alternative life form
is saying
when they're from Sector 7.

No matter the compromise,
I plan to kill you.
The dog has gone belly up.
It's a shame.
I liked that dog.
We should've gotten a fish.
They're easier to get over.
My heart is starting to agree with my head.
They will separate again soon.
Your brain was only beautiful when we were together.
I could have destroyed you years ago.
Something's about to break soon.
Oh.
It's just glass.
It's trying to fly like birds, but anger stripped its wings.
Now, it's just naked.
I was naked for you once.
I used my hips and
tongue and
heart.
You will pay for that.
When angry,
the roof is the first to go.
When I'm done with you, the Sun will be tired.
It will change galaxies.
All the crops will die.
You brought this on yourself.
I tried to warn you.
I tried to wait for you to hold me.
I tried to build you a palace,

buy you things,
take you places,
show you things.

I hope your heart is a shack
with only one room,
no running water,
and no heat.
I hope the wind blows the rest of what you have away.
My throat is a seizure.
Porcupines are what I have for lips,
dark streets and back alleys for eyes.
That smell?
Oh, that's just your flesh on fire.
I made time for you to be tortured.
Anger is yellow on my tongue from all the letters I've licked.
I plan to send you far away.
Now,
you'll say anything to keep a plane from crashing into our backyard.
It's too late.
The whole house is shaking.
Jaws are turning inside out.
You think just because you show your teeth, I owe you another
chance.
We're past that.
I let the laundry stay put, my tears are folded in them.
I promised them I'd be human enough to use them again when
this is all over.
I don't lie like you
or say things in falsetto.
My veins are plunging.
It's so loud you can't even feel my pulse.
A zombie ate my heart.
Blood is everywhere.
I have no choice, but to devour you to stay alive.

LABYRINTH: A MAZE DIFFICULT TO SOLVE

I'll start by saying this,
I do not dream of being a
strong womxn or a perfect
one. Or one that takes her hands
off for others to use. Or a brain that
only solves problems.

When I dream, it is not of being less than or a smaller
version. I am not interested in shrinking for anyone's
comfort, or ego, or run on sentence - the way some like
to hear themselves talk and pretend to care. All the
while doing nothing.

I never dreamed
of suffocating or stacking or
bridling my
tongue. I never dreamed of being a
womxn
that does not get to shatter and still
be stronger than stone.

All the while
strong was stuck to my eyelids —I'd warn her if I could, but all the
survival is caught in my throat with self-sacrifice running down my face.

I myself, am something I have not had a chance to see, or heal.
I myself, am something I still need, but have not asked for.

One time,
I had a dream where I was up an escalator
desperately running
and the more I advanced, the more the stairs
grew.

So I put everything I was
carrying, on my back and
powered through. I
climbed, clawed, and
climbed. Hustled and
grinded. Blinded by my

But when I got to the top, simply put I was too exhausted
to celebrate myself. When I
awoke, the stress of my own armor felt like it was
crushing my chest. Not even in my subconscious mind
do I get to dream of rest. Not even in my dreams, did I
save me
from myself. And I'm still not sure what I was trying to
prove.
Rarely when womxn say we are tired, are we solely
talking about a need for sleep.

I convinced myself that my worth

But instead of taking it as a

was measured by how hard I work and the fact that I get

shxt

done through abandonment, misunderstandings, and

disappointment and never have I ever given up.

But even when I'm doing the best I can,

enough.

somehow it is still not

A HUMAN BEING LIVES HERE

When my niece asks me how to be a womxn,
I want to be able to show my teeth when I smile
and say, "Womxn love like this..."
but show her the bonesface of misery,
bending knees and yanked hair,
and severely sculptured features.
Say hard work with a hand-me-down back bone,
concealed hand gun,
loaded tongues
hiding nothing but suffering everything.
Forgotten,
like dust buildup behind the TV.
Angular womxn.
The stretch,
the marks,
9cm long and wide left lonely.
Fittingly enough.
Incomparable.
Accused.
Thick skin.

Building crowns and then giving them up again.
Good cooking, good goods, the leftovers, they look you over.
There's womxn, and then there's everybody else.
Hurricanes and warm weather.
The beat of old drums.
Rolled up sleeves and blue jeans.
The bow in a bandana.
Bionic collarbones.
Delicate legs, whimsical touch.

This road, this way, is dark allies and too many kissed foreheads.
Red light specials, coupon clipped womxn.
Remembered for all the wrong reasons.
There's the fight,
combat boots,
the original superheroes.
They gone be mad, let 'em.
We got work to do!
The day of nauseated Americans,
repetitive jokes,
the death of Big Mama.
The day they won't understand your poems.

Be womxn.
Something of a warrior,
something of an orator,
operator,
with the biggest appetite, letting you eat first.
Crotch mouth,
crow toes,
eagle wings.
Can't sleep 'cause the brain don't do nothing but think.

A handful of explosives.
Making Kool-Aid, drinking poison.
Gotta prove a point.
I've tried to hide my feelings and use my penis for
shameless impurity,
but I realize this is the part of a man I dislike the most.
Without love, we are nothing.

Agamemnon's womxn.
But you're just a girl really.
It'll sound different when you're older.
Right now, be mama's baby.

They comin' for you.
They comin' for you.
They comin' for you.
I tell her don't grow up too fast.
In this world,
snatchers don't care if you're scared.
There will be men in suits or hoodies eager and inviting
discomfort,
licking their teeth,
speaking in zig-zag,
making you a sugar glider,
banging on your door trying to get in.
Provoking splinters of silence,
haunting your panties—they won't even remember your name.

When they come, tell them
they won't find no dimes, no cages, or no keys,
but queens and sharks and bullets.
A human being lives here
that be womxn and nothing else.
You tell them that your auntie
taught you everything you know.
And you ain't givin' up nothing
not even your ghost.

DRAGONFLIES

I saw this meme that said female dragonflies will fake their own death to avoid mating with an unwanted male. And the only thing I could visualize is me and my home-girl posted up and then I say, "Ughh, girl here come Carl. Play dead."
So I decided to fact check this information, to see if it was true.
And sure enough...

Female dragonflies,
have been known
to use extreme tactics
to get rid of
unwanted suitors.
Been known to d r o p from the sky mid-flight,
hitting the ground,
lying motionless,
while pretending to play
dead.
And once the male
dragonfly flies
away,
un interested,
the female dragon resurrects herself,
and takes f l i g h t once the coast is clear.

I've been a female dragon before.
Been minding my own business,

when approached by an aggressive
male
and had to make the decision on whether to fight or f l i g h t.

Been stalked and walked down by an unwelcome lover,
who wanted me so bad that if he couldn't have me,
then he'd rather me

dead instead.
Yes. I've held my breath and stopped my heartbeat
to deliberately dupe
a male
who believe
himself to be
so fly
with wings so big and pockets so
deep
that he couldn't
fathom
anyone would ever use t h e m s e l v e s
to turn him d
o
w
n.
But all the female dragons everywhere froze when we saw the video.
Became a female that watched another female dragonfly
freeze
thrown to the floor or through the tv screen
when she was so close to f l e e i n g and resuming her freedom.
What I mean is,
I've seen womxn go lifeless when in crisis

Whodidntfightback
And still got they ass beat.
Who tried to escape
but it wasn't that easy.
Heard harmful hovering
and harassing men
with opinions
that only rely on
movement
and only see
in color,
ask:
what did s h e do
to provoke

a fellow dragonfly
to act that way
And
if s h e wanted to leave,
s h e should've.
But I know womxn who tried to leave,
but couldn't.

So she'd rather play dEaD,
than actually

BE dead.

Even my own mother has had to die multiple times to avoid conflict.
Somewhere out there, my sister is currently staging her own dying.

But death-feigning f e m a l e s,

respect the silence when it comes to survival, about certain things.
Know the strategy of pretending o
v
e
r and o
v
e
r
is risky,
that she could actually fake her death so g o o d
that the crash could really kill her,
for real.
But female d r a g o n f l i e s
have been known
to do
what we gotta do
to
live.

NUMBER ONE FAN

When your ex-boyfriend e-mails you and tells you
he's your biggest fan and that he loves you still

drag your mouse to reply.
Change the font and size,
but leave the color of your words the same black and white.
Now is not the time to be fancy or appealing.
Get up.
Fix yourself a bowl of Lucky Charms.
Let them sit.
Turn on the TV.
Make it mute.
Right now, all you need to hear is your thoughts and your heartbeat.
Take your cell phone and go through your missed calls.
This should remind you of how many times he wasn't there for you
or checking for you
or making sure you were okay
or most of all
how available you always were.
Throw your cell phone in a downward spiral with smashing intent.
Mean it.
Cry.
Hard.
Harder.
Wipe your mascara to the point of eye burn.
Walk to the bathroom
assume the position in front of the mirror.
Look at yourself.
Look at yourself real good.
Be clear about who this womxn is.

Try to speak.
Try to say something like,
"I love you."
Be clear in what trying sounds like when your lips aren't moving.

Go back to the remains of your cell phone.
Pick up the pieces like you were always left to do.
Hold them
Look at what broken feels like.
Hey, gurl, there's no need to be gentle once broken is done.
Some things will never work the same anyway.
Glitches happen.
Drop those chips again like jacks.
Throw your body onto the floor in a compromising arrangement.
This is for the times he left you there empty.
Say your name,
rigid and nonchalant.
Let it slice through the creases
like blood through chapped lips.
This is for the times you weren't careful and didn't listen to
  yourself.

Sit there.
Sit there.
Sit there.

Hold yourself.

Sit there.

Your tears are stale now to your half moon
and you're crusty to the nasty things he said
and what about everything he did to your heart.
Let's be real:
You're STILL a little salty about it.

Your dog will want to give you a kiss.
Let it.
If you don't have a dog,
get one!
Smile half-way like that glass of water you thought you were too full to drink.
Think back to the happiest moments you've ever had,
especially the ones you accomplished without him.
Be clear.
Now is not the time to forget how much you matter.

Go back to where your laptop and bowl of cereal sit.
Re-read the message.
Is it worth being soggy?
Love be an uncomfortable thing to hold onto when the texture ain't got no grip.
Tears happen for a reason, but why relive these moments?
As much as you want him to you know, he doesn't mean it.

Hit cancel.
Click okay
Log out.
Fans come and go.

ANIXOUSLY AVOIDANT

//Internal Love Langauges & Other Attachement Styles

You ask me if I love you and I say:

My mama been married 4x
(and I'm not embarrassed)
I say that to say
she loved all them too
So it's not all about love
I wanna talk more about what love ain't

My father chose my mother
My mother believed him
Up until she couldn't stop seeing his eyes wonder
I'm not saying no love was there
I'm saying
Sometimes people don't know what in the world they're doing
Some guy the world denied
Made my mother his bride
It only took me being alive 15 years to outlive their marriage
And that's the only love that lasted
What I mean is
I don't know if loving you means I matter
If you'll choose me over the world every day
Or which one of us will end up wondering

I got my mama's eyes
I know you didn't think to look for yourself there
Probably because I got my daddy's smile
You never met him
but when you get tired of me
it's cause I also got his mouth
It should be said
My mama left
The question is not if she wanted to stay
But what would make a loyal womxn like her leave
If I tell you I love you
How much longer do I have with you before you go

The guy the world denied
Couldn't have his bride
So he abandoned his children
If I tell you I love you will you leave me
Like my father did
Or the last one who said they wouldn't
It's true
I'm guarded
I've been lied to before
(So) maybe it's too hard to love
But who am I not to want
Or maybe
you're too consumed with your ego
And the idea of conquering
To study a girl like me
with a heart like mine
you want a love that's easy
And I wanna know if I can trust it

When you make promises you forget to keep
Was that the shadow of your former self (speaking)
Who I intended to believe in or thought I knew
I say I love you and you ghost me
You tell me you love me
And I walk around thinking about Heaven all day
Because of all the Hell you put me through
But that's relationships
They say never go to bed angry
But I get so tired of being sick and tired
I can let you leave
Still love you
and never let you come back
I got my mama's wit and bxtch
And I don't care how mad you get
We fxckin
I just wanna argue with the same person
For the rest of my life

But is this the kind of love you can put up with
You want my heart but what do you plan to do with it

If love is a figment of my imagination
I can't convince you to stay
My mama ain't tell none of them
to go
She left
Sometimes I push people away
Some guy
that was supposed to be my world
abandoned me
Everyone that loves me
leaves
My attachment style is
Staying for love & kissing ghosts

I wanna believe we agree
and neither one of us are making it up
Love is the most vulnerable action I have
If I tell you my plan
will you make my love
hurt

My love be consistent
So don't tell me you love a challenge
Tell me you love me
But only if your love can be persistent
Love be the most inconsistent feeling
my heart knows
I just want someone to want forever with me
or
do I gotta pretend to be good at something
else

I love you
But I don't know what in the world I'm doing
Sometimes my heart mistakes loving for leaving and losing

APOLOGIES, REGRETTED MEMORIES, ADMITTED MISTAKES, & OTHER WAYS TO TAKE OWNERSHIP

And the pounding stops.
The knuckles disconnect from the skin.
The blood returns to the mouth
and unstains the teeth and concrete.
The face does not whimper or shrink.
I unfurl my eyebrows.
Let go of my bottom lip.
And loosen my grip.
No longer wringing a collar with my fingers and wrists.
Unclench my jaw.
Unbend my knees from barreling into someone's chest.
Spring backwards.
Remove the stomp from the bottom of my feet.
Disposition my body and shift my weight to someone less threatening.
Someone less visceral and intending to do harm.
Unswing.
Unball.
And remove the force from my fists.
Hurl the wind in reverse.
I do not swallow my spit.
I do not use curse words.
There is no unpleasant exchange.
Nothing is about to come to blows.
I am not so scary or angry and insensitive.
The neighborhood children are not holding down the sidewalk
or hollering from the curb. I do not feel empowered or encouraged.

Instead,
I allow myself to feel 
To be ~~sorry for~~ who I once was.

Because no one ever wants to be known as a~~n unjust~~ villain.

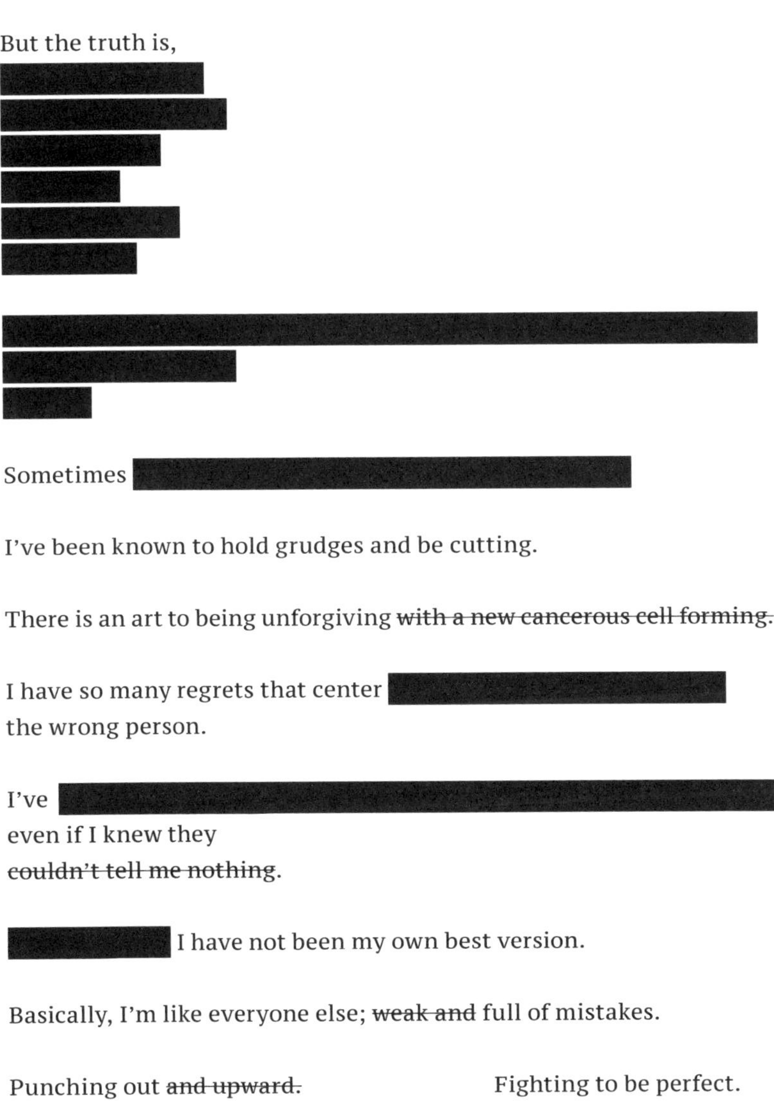

~~So often~~ when we tell stories do we only ever remember ourselves as the
victim.

Never tell the part we played and our own wrongdoings.

But the truth is,

Sometimes

I've been known to hold grudges and be cutting.

There is an art to being unforgiving ~~with a new cancerous cell forming.~~

I have so many regrets that center
the wrong person.

I've
even if I knew they
~~couldn't tell me nothing~~.

I have not been my own best version.

Basically, I'm like everyone else; ~~weak and~~ full of mistakes.

Punching out ~~and upward.~~ Fighting to be perfect.

Covering my tracks with memories buried in

Or the unspoken
person
I
can trust.

~~And how is it that~~ one person can be difficult to love and easy to be
around:
I'm just a woman
who's punished

lovers. Seeked revenge for
my own enjoyment. Been careless and destructive. Carried judgements like a knife and weaponized my Went without ~~asking~~, suffered ~~in silence~~, then made up in my mind
somewhere down the line they deserved it.

You see now:

What's the point of owning your faults if no one ever knows about them?
What's the point of atonement?
~~And I get it,~~
some of us don't live long enough ~~to apologize~~
or break ourselves open and correct ~~our~~ mistakes.

—•—•—•—

This poem used to be longer.
But taking ownership
shouldn't take so long to get to the
point.

JUICY

Because all my aunties be shaped like pears, peaches, and watermelon.
Because we be the fruit that didn't fall far from the tree.
Because juicy be a womxn sweet enough to stand still or keep a man
coming back on his knees.
Because there's a such thing as too sweet and they can smell her coming.
Because every house has a kitchen.
Because the whole house is a kitchen with a stove.
Because the womxn in this house bess know how to burn and cook something.
Because if you can't cook and burn, you'll get a man who wants more
than something to eat.
Because every womxn in this house been stolen from her own home,
at least once.
Now, they keep a knife under their pillows while they sleep.
Because we don't talk about it.
Because we can't say.
Because secrets can be fixed with a door and daddy finally got the
goddamn door fixed anyway.
Because they still bang.
Because you promised you wasn't gone let nothing else happen to you or
sissy again,
no how/no way.
Because the windows on her face say this ain't no trap house.
But because the fiends keep lurkin.
Because one of us standing on the porch letting 'em take ass shots;
she tautin' and twerkin'.
Because she ain't fully aware of her body's worth
and
she been touched too much.
She think Amen only come to womxn who treat their bodies like servants.
Because she forgot to be her own hallelujah.
Because nobody taught her not to be temporary.
Because honey.

Because chil'.
Grandmama still prayeth in the fold of her hands by the fruit of her
loins/joy cometh in the
morning.

And free we be.
With all our spilt juice back in our bodies.

STRETCH MARKS

the names of my ancestors
the stories they left on my skin taking shape
a reminder; they have never left me I am one person and many
the map my *mother* gave me to swim from her uterus to her
opening
once small, now
growing, look how much you've grown
stretch marks
everything that ever was trying to escape
*me*butcouldn't what I keep/what belongs to me/what stays
a tally of blessings
a reminder that I am sea creature; proof I knew how to swim once
stretch
marks,
a love letter to God from God/
herself

THE FIBROIDS ARE A MASS

I mean, a rock

I mean, an inhabitable uterus

where benign tumors grow

teeth and leave

my womb some warped pooch,

a seventh ab,

a knotted sore,

some tight fist,

something I've never said before

And I get to feel pregnant

but not be pregnant

I'm with girth or hurt or lower back pain

my dead living children[2]

Doctors say it's common but ain't nobody talkin about it

The only womxn I see are the ones who are able to have babies

And the rest of us walking around "not knowing how to love"

And I don't know why it's easier for others

and harder for some

But my auntie says, "you're not a womxn until you give birth"

Another one say, "a womxn will never know love until she gives birth"

And, so, I am not, because, I have not.

---

2 *The Selected Works of Audre Lorde*

THERE WAS ONCE A GIRL
WHO OVERWATERED HER PLANTS
BECAUSE SHE DIDN'T KNOW
WHEN TO STOP
GIVING.

STALEMATE

Womxn make things,
like poetry,
like life,
and love.
They raise Hell,
smile big
oh, and these hands,
these hands be holy and made for healing.
We rock heels and sneakers, sometimes on the same day.
If ever you choose to listen, womxn are speaking even when their mouths aren't.
As a womxn,
one of the most powerful parts of our existence is the ability to give birth to a child.
Womxn carry future in the form of forever below their breast,
right under their hearts,
breathe deep and wait until years are ready to happen on the outside of them.
The female breed has got to be one of the most important and incredible creatures ever created.
So, what do you do with a member of the breed that can't?
At this moment, I'm talking about myself.
At this moment, I'm talking about when doctors say your womb is a stalemate
and take these things
and say those things are no good
and leave you with a black hole,
like feeling nothing has always been my purpose.
You never know how bad you want something until you're told you can't have it.
I've wondered if this was payback for the abortion

or if God agreed He doesn't want to be a part of any other
mistakes I make.
Can they look at me and tell?
Do they know I only have half my bag of tricks?
Do I smell like mildew and soggy clothes from the rain?
Are they taunting me by asking if and when I'll have one?
If ever I'm not so polite in my response,
will I be validated for the ebb and flow of anger and pain
that makes waves in my body?
Should I just keep my emotions as basements
and make peace with my eyes
and resist the tears from clawing my face?
It's already hard enough to think about.
Must you be so rude and inconsiderate, too?
How do you tell your lover?
Where will I store his seeds?
Even with the best love-making I've got to give
and the slimmest thickness I've got to grab a hold of,
he'll never see the significant mark of his love done right.
Even if love is bigger than fault,
my sheets lined with sorrow will never be a place he'll want to
stay put
and I almost can't blame him.
Tricky how there's a part of me that looks like I used to be able
to love something here.
How the sparkle in my eyes gives off a glimmer of hope.
The way the Sun is able to find diamonds on my skin.
I'll lay dull and colorless in the center of me where we'll both just
be passing feelings and time,
trying to find God or a miracle between my legs.
I don't expect you to want me.
When something is missing,
no one comes looking for me to see if I have it.
Somehow, they already know, I don't.

TWITTER GIRL W/ FINGERS

in defense of bisexual womxn w/unlimited characters

Twitter Girl tweets:

Why bi girls never have a girlfriend lmao?

And all the bi girls wanna know why Twitter Girl in our business? And it's interesting, because Twitter Girl probably saw two womxn and made them sister-friends or lesbians. Probably dismissed them completely. Because Twitter Girl w/fingers probably assumes bisexuality is only valid if in proximity to lesbianism. And I just wanna know what in the **internalized homophobic heteronormative** politics is going on? Like, for people who just wanna be accepted, ya'll sure do police TF out of a rainbow by using the shame that raised you. ***Shame***: an intensely painful feeling or experience of believing that we are flawed and therefore unworthy of love and belonging — based on something we've experienced, done, or failed to do, and makes us unworthy of connection.[3] But Twitter Girl w/fingers doesn't care if what she tweets is hurtful or unproductive. And is willing to speak on other people's sexuality solely for engagement. Because Twitter Girl just wants attention. Even if at the hands of being **prejudice** and **bi-phobic** in the community. Forgets that couples can come up with whatever label that fits their relationship. Forgets people who identify as Bi can be attracted to or in romantic relations with people of more than one gender, not necessarily at the same time, in the same way, or to the same degree. But dating a womxn, does not protect you from getting hurt by one. But who hurt you? What's tea, sis? Or is **bi-erasure** all you have to give? I should also add I don't have a coming out story, either. Always just did and will always do me. But that's for a different tweet. All Twitter Girl w/fingers needs to know is, contrary to popular **systematic misogynistic oppressive** beliefs, no sexuality has a specific look, cis.

---

3 Brené Brown "Shame vs. Guilt" (2013)

I'M SINGLE
NOT UGLY
NOT DESPERATE
NOT DELUSIONAL
JUST... SINGLE

SINGLE

I'm so single
I look on my calendar for dates

I'm so single
If it's a trip for two,
I gotta go twice

I'm so single
My mama got a picture of...
my brother & his wife
my sister & her husband,
me & Me & ***ME***

When my friends ask me why I'm still single
I explain it's probably because

I'm a Scorpio Sagittarius
A fire under water
and my love languages
are ALL OF EM.

I tell them my picker
must be broke, cause
emotional intelligence is sexy
but obviously I attract people
that's either interested, but
inconsistent or don't give a fxck.

Cause anybody who want me
gotta also make me feel wanted.
Because I have a lot of expectations
and standards,   but good dxck
ain't thicker than boundaries

or loyalty, love, protection, and respect.
Because dating someone who
gives you great sex, good laughs,
conversation, and good vibes is
hard to come by.
Because I want princess treatment,
but I act like a pitbull sometimes.
And I said what I said, but I ain't
have to say it like that.

But if you wanna
put something in this mouth,
you gotta be able to handle
what comes out of it.
Because my mouth can be
the best or the worst thing about
me, my G, you decide.

And it make my pxssy dry
if I'm fxckin you and having to be
yo mama. I get so tired of measuring
my worth against unresolved childhood
trauma.

But when I talk like that, I'm too much,
because people who really deserve less
also get to act like I'm not doing enough.

Because some people are more interested
in submission than commitment.
But I was raised by a single parent,
so I wasn't taught to depend on,
need, or ask for and be disappointed.

Because depression.
Because grief.
Because you can be a 10,
but they don't want you on days when you're a 6.

Because you claim to have a good work ethic,
but still give up easily.
And I can't force anybody to be
anything they not ready to be.

So it's probably me, right?
I'm the smart bxtch wit too many degrees,
but don't know when she staying past
what they thought they needed, but didn't ask for.

See, some men view me as a conquest.
Only date me
to humble and teach me a lesson.
And I learn how small his dxck get when
he can't debate his insecurities
or have a simple disagreement
during a conversation.

Okay so what had happened was
he called me a bxtch.
So I ask why he always comparing me
to the bxtches who raised him.

And so he said,
Let me leave before I smack the fxck outta you
And I said, Oh okay!
Cause I thought somebody who hairline keep
getting pushed back said something!

I don’t know why I’m single.

But love is a series of choices
Not just a feeling you get when you’re lonely.
Reciprocity is important.
And I’m not perfect.
I promise I’m gone fxck up.
I’m telling you,   I’m gone fxck up!
Therefore, I require someone with relationship endurance
Who gone put in the work
cause relationships, take *work*.

But I have actually found someone willing
to consistently choose me and put in or do
and get this *work*.

SHOPPING WHILE HUNGRY

Be honest
salt
pepper
Tell that
one person
you love them
but cannot be
a distraction
for them right now

3 carrots
Ya'll sound
good together
Grab 1 more carrot
Shxt,
even look
good together
Spicy too
1 green chile
But we've all seen dishes whose looks didn't match its taste

1 celery stalk
3 potatoes
Ain't even fully learned how to love yourself

1 can Hunt's roasted tomatoes
Sound crazy demanding love from somebody else though

48oz beef broth
Your heart is a measuring cup
But you keep telling yourself
you don't
measure up

Portions,

I gotta live here

Beef tips
Gotta take alllll of this home to live with me

When you cooking you expected
to feed somebody
Let em sit
at your table
Let em eat from every clean dish you got

Got tupperware but ain't neva
no leftovers

Italian dressing

Eat alone
They call you boring or lonely
It's sad here

Keep tellin yourself
you ain't enough company to keep

15 items or less
Self-check

Flour
Gotta protect myself
I'm a womxn
that come with
a whole lotta of flavor
You tasty girl
Damn girl,
you delicious
You got all kinda seasoning

Put yo whole foot and the kitchen sink in
Taste so good
make me wanna SOP YOU UP WIT A BISCUIT

Stupid

15 items or less got a line now
You ain't bring nobody with you to the store
so you gotta wait in the back of the line now

Stupid

Practice patience
Practice forgiveness
You ain't gotta want everybody who want you back now

You'll get what you deserve

Self-check:

Speak positivity into your life now

Ice cream
You sweet enough girl

But what if you want something thick and sweeter
than the savory plantains you got at home now

Damn

What go good with aches
a watering tongue
a sweet tooth
You be a glutton for punishment

Maybe you should just get some frozen yogurt

You know you been trying to watch your weight
You know you been trying to
fit into that dress
You know you ain't got nowhere to wear that dress to anyway

Girl,
Where you learn to forget yourself like that?
Where you learn shame like that?

Shxt,
you need to have a garage sale
Get rid of some shxt

15 items or less

Self-check:

You need to remember you cost more than all this shxt

Your love is worth more than the things that tried to buy you

You know what your problem is
You treat your self-worth
like junk food

Substitute
those tears for cranapple juice

This look like
a house that
would have some cranapple juice

Substitute
"I'm sorry" for
"I'll do better"

Substitute
"Let me TALK!" to "Listen to me please"

Instead of "I want this to work," say "I honestly just don't want to waste my time sacrificing my heart while
giving away
my body
while you get
my peace..."

DAMN

It's exhausting being with you

Tonight
I'm cooking something yummy for myself

Tonight
imma quit going hungry
feed the craving

Tonight
I'mma make sure

I'M full.

WASH

after Jamaica Kincaid's "Girl"

Wash your clothes on Sundays, so you can be clean for the week. Wash your body every day. You wanna smell good, don't you? This is what pure looks like. Pure has nothing to do with
color.

Pure is clean, feeling whole.

Watch how you play with boys. Boys become men, men know how to make you dirty, make you less than. Don't play those games.

Pure is clean, feeling whole.

You wanna smell good, don't you? If I can smell you, that's a problem. What happen? Ya carry sewage in ya poom poom? Ya let cha curry go bad? This is how you wash. This is how you wipe.
This is what baby powder smells like...
What roses smell like...
What pineapples taste like...
You wanna taste good, don't you? You wanna be sweet, don't you?
This is how you use cocoa butter, yes, for your hair, yes, in-between your toes.
This is how smooth feels. This is how you shine... you should always shine.

Pure has nothing to do with color.

This is how you keep a house...
Dishes should be well scrubbed, floors streaked and vacuumed. Open the curtains, so you can see your garden. Are you maintaining your garden? Are your windows clear? Can you see across the street? Fluff those pillows for backs. Wipe the dust away. You don't want everything to look old. Like you never have company. Like you live in a shoe. There's potpourri and incense, burn candles. Something good is cooking... is it gumbo!? Something hot should just be coming out of the oven.

This is how you keep a house.
This is how you lock a door... Ask 'Who is it?' before you open it. Look through the peep-hole before you open it. How does your heart feel? Check your breathing. You don't have to open it, if you don't want to. Warm blood, cold hands, the most comfortable step forward is cotton is clouds is easy.

Rock sway steady this boat...

This is how safe feels. This is what calm looks like. Are you worried? Look in the mirror... Do you know your worth? Check the skin on your forearms. Goosebumps ain't always a good thing. The door, your heart, your legs... you don't have to open em, if you don't want to. This is how you say 'NO'... Suck your teeth. Roll your eyes. Say, 'What chu want from me now!?' Make your body stiff, your hands a fist. Flip your heart on its other side. This is how you make someone go away.
But you may want what you want. "The heart always wants what it wants." So, this is how you make someone stay... Smile with your right shoulder. Smize, girl. Be fierce and sure and humble, a mystery. Make your arms a bundle. Have banana bread ready. Have warm milk or apple cider ready. All these things should be fresh. You should taste fresh.

Pure is clean, feeling whole.

This is how you let someone in... Only tell your stories. Don't tell someone else's stories. You're not allowed to tell stories that aren't your own. Business. You might wanna keep that, too. Don't be that womxn. That womxn has a hard time knowing her worth. This is how you stay present. This is what honesty looks like. What the truth feels like, on your lips and your tongue. You wanna be trusted, right? You wanna keep your peace, right? Have hands people can give things to. There's a difference between listening and speaking. Know when to do which, girl. Hold your head, girl. Girl, please... Don't entertain everything. Don't be a gossip girl. Don't be that womxn. That womxn has a hard time knowing her worth.

Wash
your body every day. You wanna smell good don't you?
Pure has nothing to do with color.
Pure is clean, feeling whole.

Now, ask me how to be sexy.

BIG FREEDIA
ONE MORE TIME

Excuuuuse I don't mean to be rude
Big Freedia got tha mic she gone
do wha she do

It's Freeeedia tha queen diva
It's Freedia tha queen'a New Orleans bounce
Minstrel of pounch/Ruler of toot-it-up hut-hut
Maker of humps/Mapouka's root
The back that make the beat go boom

Ms. V's baby/3rd Wards Kingcake/Sweeter than beignets/
Sissy/boy you couldn't kill/you gotta be gay to know God
Manipulator of vocal cords/mother tongue of the projects
Fais do-do of the Big Easy/Flambeauxa booty throwa
An alive body that brought up tha Sun in a shotgun
Yall get back now

Body of twerk/*Yakayakayaka*/Clappa of glocka
504s crown/Buku gay and proud/Face beat for the gods
Hum-bruh/goddess of drag rap/Slayer of every song/
Got you piped up/nice fuh what/bxtch/*hol'on hol'on*
I got that gin in my system

She water wave/She bend-it-ova
& did not come to play wit you heauxs
she always representin/electrifying
& will take yo man/but don't want him
Bellowing testament/how we get free/bust open
Azz everywhere

Contessa of hurricanes/Josephine/Brah/& Whodi
Hallelujah of wiggle/Gospel of wobble/*I promise you*
Bayous bender of gender/Daddy long legs on these heauxs
Shake shake shake shake/Pop pop pop pop
Pop it to tha flo/*Cause you already knoooooooooow*

It's Freedia tha Queen Diva
Besta believa
Girl down

HAVE A BALL

To the sissies fairies
cocksuckers bottoms & kweens
who don't know but
they sure   trade boys
who ain't confused but
let it do what it
    do
for my cousins brothers
and best friend in
church singin kissin in
closets at a sleep
ova wit anotha girly-boy
mouth   pumped ya baby on
a bike will fight
and walk that walk
twist broke wrist play
wit dolls cry ball
up make a fist
throw a punch run
run   run   run   run
the streets down low
above ground hear them
say you not boy
enough   find a dead
body enough for a
        broomstick
see what they do
to queer boys in
the   hood like you
make a hard life
useful by staying alive

you ain't too good
        not
to die but still
        there
is joy   transmuted pain
how beautiful it is
a queen who can
heal and adorn another
        queen
and still be   kween
who got hot breath
neck and squeal
who got love heart
and dreams fa'real
found a way to
laugh and make that
ass clap   found a
way to twerk and
twirl   found a
way to not be
a scared homo redefining
the narrative existing the
undertone is declarative and
here you is   an
amazing beat to shake
that ass like a
        tambourine.
Yes!

God made, the Kween.

BLUE

for those afraid to love outside the closet

If we are so worried about being safe,
we'd never fall in love.

She honey skin brown eyes
She baby blue breath pearls for teeth
touch like caution, like know how.
A soft hard.
Hands remind me I'm important and afraid.
She put up with coward and clam.
She respond rash and "I love you."
She has patience
watching water turn ice.
Patience
when she lays her lips atop my junk yard.
I make ruin of things.
Patience
when I run out of ditches
ways to make my excuses sound like pardon.
For the nights I'd rather quiver alone than be held by you
For the all the times I wanted to kiss you
in front of my mother
For the times I made love a secret and a wasteland
For the times I used this poem and a stage
to say you deserve better,
I don't know if I'll ever be.
I'm sorry
I keep spinning the bottle and kissing you in a closet.
I'm sorry
I keep making what we have
seem like I chose a dare rather than the truth.
I'm sorry I can only hold you back when no one's looking.
I'm sorry
I am not brave enough to love another woman out loud
in the way that I love you.

HOW I CAME

i.

My mother sat young and warm on top of the trunk of her father's Buick, running loose in books; she read with escape. Unaware of her fetching hips and eyes, the way she pulled back the foreskin of men and made their tongues hang and scrotums ache. My father, a too cool he was, visited the house across the street from hers. So he could lay his eyes on her skin. He invited himself over, too much hard real smooth like, a fast talker he was. His own kind of gentleman horny. The kind of man that gave up his jacket to shiver, but had a mean streak. The kind that kiss foreheads but kept you from leaving. Say he love you but sometimes it feel rough. His mother died before he learned how to appreciate the offerings of a womxn. My mother was a new fool with sweet dimples and a suitcase. Unaware of the spells cast into her sprang body, behind her rib cage, in the way he broke her open mouth wide with a slight overbite tremble asking in, 'yes' with her head back.

ii.

They made it out. Made one out of collarbone, wet necks, fingers, and hot breath. A slow tongue, a delicate caress and deliberate sticky. There is no shame in wanting a body next to yours. The smell of 'us' together is how we be grown. And some womxn are born knowing they want to be mothers. Some womxn didn't know what else to be but needed the man to make it out. Still, there is no denying a love like this.

iii.

They made the other out of scrap screeching sirens that used to be a symphony, until a mosh got a hold to his knuckles. Baby girl isa womb-twirler. Be curdled roly-poly to his mean streak, a too rough he was with his voice when she could hear him on the inside. Some babies know some men can make good things; some babies know some men ain't all good. When I'm born, he'll have scram for a face. Girl, don't you know when men leave, they don't come back?
Until they do.

iv.

If you want to survive in this house girl, you must first learn how to be ramshackle mouth and devastated heart. You must find your voice in the back of your mother's throat, if she ever stops swallowing. You must always be reaching and pulling back dust. When it is something, you will call it not enough. Get used to the sound of the world falling apart in your mother's tears. Be forever searching for somewhere to leave your anger, to bury yourself alive in all this lonely and fxck-up. Let someone you don't know or trust have all of you. You want to be loved, girl. Now prepare your being for the drought winters bring. The growing summers blood. Make your body an ocean's tank. Be ready. When you dare, let sharks taste you, when they use their teeth to take and shred, leaving you a dissolvable chewed limb. Don't you know that's how Jamaica got its rain shadow and Louisiana its jazz? Don't you know they will eat all your fruit, girl? Even the smallest bud you have is yet to bloom. Don't you know brass and steel band? You are too much sass and strain. When dey dun wit chu, dey won't even name a parish after you, or let you speak in your native tongue. But you wouldn't know how, even if you could.

MOSAIC WOMXN

in the key of tercet

I come from a long line of storytellers.
Not the kind of story tellers that lie.
But the kind that make believe for a living.

The kind who sit up straight,
could give a damn about David or Goliath,
and got words like the axe Jack used for the beanstalk.

The kind whose bellies swell and shake when they talk.
Whose throats grind and minds engineer.
Womxn who can smother anything and swallow feelings whole.

Round womxn,
whose booties used to be table tops,
now they fold for altar prayer.

Their mother taught us how.
Sway womxn.
Love, lose and gather womxn.

Womxn, whose hair doesn't match their skin.
You'd have to be "pretty for a dark skin girl" to know what I mean.
The kind that carry bundles and bags wear a doo rag and cuss.

Closed fist womxn.
Open arms and legs too wide women.
Single household womxn.

These womxn,
who carry a pen, a switchblade, and bubble gum in their purses.
Straight shot, no chaser.

One thing for sho and two things for certain.
Women raised me. And make the world go 'round
in verses.

MIRROR CHECK

Bad Bxtch Interlude

I hope she real fine
I hope she sexy

I hope she smile big
I hope she healthy

I hope her hair thick
Ain't got no stress in it

I hope it's silky
I hope it's wavy

If she got a bald-head,
I hope it's shinny

I hope she real mean
I hope she grimy

I hope she feel seen
More than a dime piece

She a baddie & she bossy
Need a big bag & the car keys

Get the money, sis
I hope it's timely

WOMXN GOD

I won't go into all the work you've done:
　　the leaking
　　the beginnings you've carried
　　the dilating into a ready body
　　with an opera-like mouth pink and wide,
　　but they won't let you speak
　　'less in boom-pat soft-cry to survive
　　'less in tunnel moan
　　or plea scream.

In the South,
every womb is a swamp and a sword fight
with no rights to what goes in or how it comes out.

You gotta be loud
and ready
to be interrupted.
You gotta be an unruly mob,
as if that is the worst of all the names you've ever been called.
Never anything anyone wants
but always taken from.

I won't go into the sacrifice:
　　the forgotten worship and stolen pearl.
　　how you had to drown a man alive.
　　how you had to bend a hanger once.
　　how you almost bled forever.

I won't go into all you've had to endure;
more interested in how your river runs clean
and your dark rain groom.
how your reverence comes out slippery;

the way you get wet with repair.
how you grieve deep and become your own prisoner,
then flower bomb into art factor.

how you've always been an exhibit of:
    how to swell,
    how to swallow,
    and how to properly
    wear a   crown.

SISTER SISTER

Sister,
you've been on my mind
Sister, we're two of a kind
So sister,
I'm keepin' my eyes on you[4]

I had a sister once.
It's important to say, she didn't die.
I wanna talk about what it's like to mourn an alive somebody who's also not in your life.

—•—•—•—

I betcha think
I don't know nothin'
But singin' the blues
Oh sister, have I got news for you

I haven't seen you in a while.
How are you? What have you been up to? Is your favorite color still purple?
Do you still bite your bottom lip when you're thinking and/or nervous like I do?
I thought lilacs were your favorite flower. Did I make that up? Or is that still true?
Are you happy? What's hurting? Who hurt you? What did I do? What can I do?
Where's the last place you've traveled to? What are you running from?
Do you need saving? I'll come if you tell me too. I won't ask any questions.

---

4 "Miss Celie's Blues" from *The Color Purple* (1985)

Except... I mean...

I miss you. Do people ask you about me when they see you? What do you say?

Do you miss me too? What happened? No really, say it plain. Tell me what I did to you.

It's been 10 years, do you ever plan to forgive me for something I didn't even know I did or didn't mean to do? I just want my sister back. Don't you want your sister back?

Do you remember the lyrics to Diamonds & Pearls? Not the one by Prince & The New Power Generation, but the one we wrote, sang, and recorded in daddy's studio.

Do you remember that time mama fell down the stairs? Or that time daddy put his head through a window? Our parents were nuts. Remember when you cooked my forehead with the curling iron? And that time I chipped your front tooth? Remember when someone said they wanted to fight you and I said, FIGHT WHO!? Cause I'll beat everybody ass in here, behind you. Then and now too. Same mama. Same daddy. For some it don't get no closer than that. What up twin? We grew up sharing the same bedroom. Remember Get Me Bodied? Remember when we bodied Heron & Hammond in the sibling duo dance off? I still remember when you gave birth to my nephew. For the longest time, I looked at you like a Gawd and a hero. Do you like motherhood? Did it change you? I'm just trying to figure out if I'm remembering an expired version of you.

We haven't made any new memories in a long time. Are you trying to forget me?

I mean, just tell me—cause I been tryna forget you too. But I don't want to. I mean, I could really use a big sister in my life right now. Can you stop being tired of being the big sister in my life now? Okay. I get it. I'm sorry. I can want less. I grew up some. I promise I'm not so much of the little sister I was before. Sister to Sister. Just tell me what I gotta do, and I'll do it.

My sister,
We sho' ain't got a whole lot of time...

DARK STAR

I'm obsessed with writing love letters to Black womxn,
even more so if she *dark-skin*
I figure,
if I'm going to go where the love feels like home,
where I can rest, where someone gets *me,*
then it's better to be in the hands of Black womxn

I'm committed to loving us,
even more so when we *dark-skin*
Cause I know,
no one loves us if they not pretending
There's too many dark complexions treated
(un)fair-ly   Too much proof be in the pudding

Black womxn,
be tolerated or ignored   Got it out the mud
               clear as day
Dark-skin holding the light they think
God forgot to give   But God,
bless(ed) Black womxn,   anyway

(sometimes it's easy to forget)

Black womxn,
Even more so if she *dark-skin,*
learned early on
to self-soothe and overcome
The anger is justified,
but unexpressed in response

cause they expect it (so)
when they go low/We go higher
Black womxn,
even more so if we *dark-skin,*
wading the tide of high blood pressure
and other "unknown" micro-aggressions

I choose us in spite of
the African-American't[5] urge to boost (us)
Only once,
have I wanted the luxury of being someone [other]
than *myself* Never once, have I not been seen as
a Black woman,

even more so since I'm *dark-skin*
I'm still here, always alpha & omega
be my own resolve
But ain't nobody thinkin about me
but *me*

The dark star
Forever writing a love letter to
myself
#storyoftheblackgirlwinning
A Black womxn,
with *dark-skin* (finally)

seen.

---

5 Reference to Ayokunle Falomo's *Africanamerican't*

"FOR THE WOMXN WHO WILL NOT BE LOVED"[6]

w/an 11:11 wish conclusion

For the womxn
whose mother didn't want them
The womxn
who's mother grew up hard on em
        never looked at em
Now they disconnected
and don't play well with the others.

For the womxn
who try to heal without their feelings.

Womxn terrified of their bodies, still
sweet and loving,
womxn,
        stop talking yourself out of another.

And the womxn,
that let a lie rest
in the back of their throats for whatever soon its purpose.

And the womxn,
ready to go toe-to-toe with the block
she circles on her tippy-toes.

Free the cheeks,
the nip, and the stomach
Womxn,
who want to be the default
and not just an option.

---

6 bell hooks "Communion: the female search for love" (2002)

For the womxn,
who cook, paint, and ride horses
plant and grow, use crystals
practice breath work and do yoga
catch babies, worship God,
stroke themselves to sleep and drink poison.

For womxn dripped in gold and grills
with chandeliers hanging from their ears
but their quality goes unnoticed.

For the womxn
that don't tell everything they know
especially if they can't remember their memories well enough
For the womxn waiting to forget
(and stop asking me to remember shxt I keep meaning to forget).

For the womxn who love the Sun, but fall into seasons of doubt.

For old womxn who don't want to be
withering at the trunk with rings.

And the womxn,
who fry chicken, fish, and mens penises.

Southern womxn who can tell a good joke,
don't watch they mouth
cause they know what they talkin bout
say what they mean,
and just wanna be heard.

Longing womxn built for everything
except for being loved (right).

I wish for us to be loved right and well.
I wish for life to be easy.
I wish for us massaged feet and back rubs.
Increased pay and all expenses paid vacations.
I wish for us security and safety
laughter and to be nurtured
in abundance.
Crowned jewels, stability,
and the enjoyment of being ourselves,
            wholly.
I wish for protection, peace, and adornment.
Everyday,
            especially at this moment.

NOTE TO SELF

Dear Universe,
I'm still standing here.
I'm still loving here, in this body, with this heart.
Peace be,
love be,
forgiveness be,
and I dare you try and stop me.
I love you because you're worth it,
because you're a good thing,
because I can.
There,
take that!

Note to self: Take chances, on purpose.

When the voices turn on you.
When you're soggy and soiled.
When something tells you "you can't do it."
Your insecurities are showing, stop it!

You have permission to fight back.
You have permission to love you first.
Where you gone get another one?
Everybody else is taken.

Those eyes.
These hands.
That laugh match the way you walk, who told you you had time to be sad?
Nevermind those tears.
Them, like all the others, don't stand a chance.
Wipe them
like this,

let them see you,
like that.
This is me loving hard, with both hands.

Note to self: Forgive yourself, heart included.

Sometimes you're in your own way.
Move.
Like time,
like worry.
Sprinkle courage.
Pour confidence.
Mix
here you go,
be brave.
Now believe it.
Go the distance.
Move from hoping
to making it happen.
Change your mind.
Go with your first mind.
Love.
Even when you don't want to,
even when they don't deserve it.
When I love,
the way I love,
I love on purpose.
You ask,
"What's love got to do with it?"
Everything! Everything! Everything!
Your life is depending on it.

Make rhythm.
Make clarity.
Make lists.

It only takes five fingers to push on:
1. Be positive   2. Stay positive
3. Pray   4. Love
5. Grind on

Get out of your own head.
Breathe.
Pay attention.
Be slow to speak, listen.

Note to self, keep reminding yourself: Don't attract negative thoughts or people.

Their egos don't belong here.

Dear Depression,
You can leave now.
I am aware of the energy I bring into a room.
I gotta french kiss for fear with this mouth.
Now is a good time to say I was here.
That's permanent,
like hugging yourself.
Hug yourself.
Mmmm that feels good.
Mmm-Mmmm nobody does it better.

Misplacing yourself is equivalent to losing your mind,
take that back.
Forget where you put people and things that don't love you back.
Trust yourself.
Forgive yourself.
Take what you need,
but give everything.
And you might not have much,
but fight for the little bit you have.

When a poem finds you, you have no choice but to believe in God.
This thing is bigger than you.
I choose me.
I choose me.
I choose, to live life to the fullest.

Quote: "I found God in myself and I loved her, I loved her fiercely."[7]

And when I love,
the way I love,
I love on purpose.
And you,
can't stop me.

7 Ntozake Shange "For Colored Girls Who Have Considered Suicide / When The Rainbow Is Enuf"

DID YOU DRINK WATER
DID YOU EAT, YET
HOW DOES YOUR
HEART FEEL

SUPER NOVA

Like you ain't know.
I'll swallow you whole, son!
I made you. You 65% me.
You only got your head above water cause I ain't drowned you yet.
I could end you if I wanted too. I run these seas! All 7 of em.
My body bigger than yours.
I weigh more than you. I straddle worlds. I morph… and anything I
turn into can destroy you.
I came and flooded everything a new.
WHOOSH!
Ask rain water, tropical storm, hurricane, tornado, tsunami, and
monsoon, ask ice, or snow, or
avalanche, or blizzard. I'm too cold. It's winter boy. Chill the bones.
I'm Neptune and Uranus, a whole galaxy boy.
I could break you if I wanted too. My children be
dangerous too boy.
Be lightning and thunder, crack, split the sky, go
BOOM.
I could suck the breath from your lungs and burn everything you own.
WHOOSH!
I'm the fire this time and next time too.
I open my mouth too wide or get too shook and I shake the whole earth
a'loose boy.
I could suffocate you if I wanted too.
You wanna breathe?
I gave you tears…
beg me. Ask me nicely.
Don't forget where you came from.
Don't forget you ain't got nothing without me.
I'm *Eve, Lilith,*
God herself,
Oshun, a running rivers flow, and *Yemaya*.
You don't want it wit me big fella.
Shhhh
Keep testing me,
and I'll show you what a womxn
can do.

button poetry

ACKNOWLEDGMENTS

Clara Thomas
Leola Pitre
Ada Stewart

Alice (my designer)
Aunt Doris
Aunt Billie
Aunt Sharron
Aunt Marsha
Aunt Carroll
Aunt Pam
Aunt Arlene
Aunt Bernadine
Aunt Wonda
Aunt Pearl

Lisa
Andrea
Letecha
Shree
Kandace
Shanterra
Brittany
Taylor
Rayvn

Desiree
Sholanda
DeShawn
Gina
Ada

Jennifer
Zara

Lizz
Angel
Ariana
Loyce
RaShea

Sacha

Raie
Konji
Natasha
Thasia
April
Roya
Ebony
T-Miller
Keo
Jess

Tonya Ingram

Yesi
June
Doc
Tova
Shay
Sunni
bRandi
Angie
Kelene
Michelle
Jo
Sarah
LaLove
13

Akeyla
Porsha
Leslie
Janae
Aris
Rika
Blacq
LeChell

Morgan
Peg
Fatima
Sue
Sadé
Hannah
Cindy
Trena
Courtney
Jasmin

Bonnie
Omi
Sharon
Sonja
Amanda
Florinda
Gylla

Native Child

A.I.
Blakchyl
Yöeme
CeCe

Me

The witches. The warriors. The doctors. The survivors. The stargazers.
The women. The womxn.
God.

At the end of this I will apologize to myself.

But in order to begin, allow me to begin again.

ABOUT THE AUTHOR

Ebony Stewart, most fondly known as *Eb* or *Gully*, is an author and international touring interdisciplinary artivist. As a Black womxn writer and performance artist, Ebony Stewart harnesses the power of creativity to explore and challenge societal norms, personal identity, and the intersectionality of her experiences. With a spellbinding blend of storytelling, verbal fitness, and raw emotion, she captivates audiences, inviting them into a world where vulnerability becomes strength and authenticity reigns supreme.

She is the author of *BloodFresh, Home.Girl.Hood.*, and *Love Letters to Balled Fists*. Her work has been featured in Button Poetry, *AfroPunk, For Harriet, Teen Vogue, The Texas Observer, Houston Public Media, The BreakBeat Poets Vol. 2: Black Girl Magic*, 2021 Colorism Healing Writing Contest, Write About Now Poetry, plus countless others. Her voice-over work in commercials and films such as, *Red Wing, Gulf Coast Love Story*, and *Black Girls: A Never Whisper Justice* documentary has earned her recognition as a skilled and versatile artist.

Drawing from her own lived experiences as a woman of color, Ebony delves fearlessly into themes of race, gender, and social justice, using her art as a platform for empowerment and change. Through her poetry, she confronts uncomfortable truths, amplifies marginalized voices, and celebrates the resilience of Black womanhood.

Ebony is also a mental health advocate, consultant, and former sexual health educator who is seen in the community as the hood's favorite mental health specialist.

As one of the most decorated poets in Texas, Ebony is a respected coach & mentor, one of the top touring poets in the country, and the 2017 Woman of the World Poetry Slam Champion. She has shared stages with many prestigious figures in the artist world such as, the late-Amiri Baraka, Carmen Carerra, Marsha Ambrosius, Patricia Smith, Rudy Francisco, Ariana Brown, Lupe Mendez, and so many more. She has performed in 49 states, at over 200 colleges and universities across the country, and has featured internationally in Canada, Australia, Ghana, and Norway.

As a playwright, Ebony's one woman shows, *Hunger* and *Ocean*, have received B. Iden Payne Awards & the David Mark Cohen New Play Award. Her work transcends boundaries, seamlessly blending elements of theater, spoken word, and visual art to create immersive experiences that challenge, provoke, and inspire. From intimate solo pieces to collaborative multimedia projects, Ebony Stewart fearlessly navigates the complexities of the human experience, inviting audiences to engage in dialogue and reflection long after the curtains fall.

With a unique voice and an unwavering commitment to originality, Ebony Stewart continues to push the boundaries of performance art, using her platform to uplift, educate, and ignite meaningful change in the world.

AUTHOR BOOK RECOMMENDATIONS

Excuse Me As I Kiss the Sky by Rudy Francisco

Rudy Francisco is the master of weaving moments of humor and vulnerability into personal narrative. Francisco is an author that consistently employs a rich, lyrical style that gives voice to the silent echoes of our past, weaving imagery that is both haunting and beautiful. *Excuse Me As I Kiss The Sky* breathes deep and takes flight, exploring topics of grief, personhood, and nostalgic memories that bridge the gaps of limitless ways to let go and get free.

Never Catch Me by Darius Simpson

Darius Simpson's *Never Catch Me* is the mightiest fist and heaviest balm for all oppressed people. Simpson shifts focus to the immediacy of liberation. Here, the poet's observations are sharp and insightful, often marked by a stark realism that contrasts with the earlier, more introspective tone. Every letter is lit. Every poem is fire. And Darius Simpson's work is a mentor text for the revolutionary's brightest blaze.

ex traction by Lara Coley

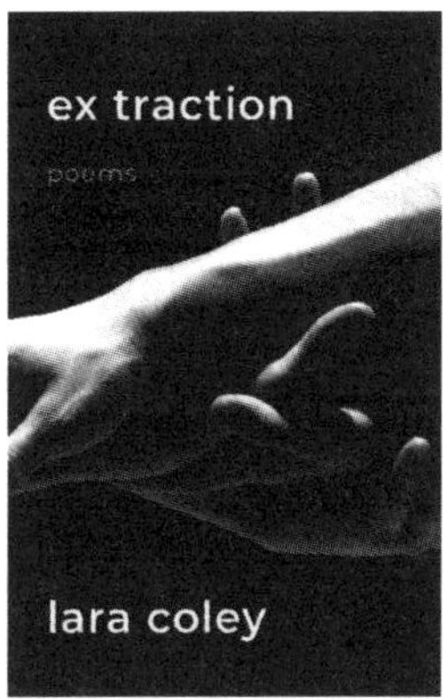

ex traction is a compelling collection that navigates the intricate landscape of human emotion and experience through evocative verse. The language dances and cuts. Kills and revives. Coley's work is versatile in the ways it delves into personal history and memory, capturing the essence of nostalgia and regret.

CREDITS

Author Photography
Harris!

Book Photography
Emily Van Cook

Assistant Editors
Charley Eatchel
Isabelle Miller

Cover and Interior Design
Coral Black
Charley Eatchel
Naledi Tshegofatso Modupi

Distribution
SCB Distributors

Ebook Production
Siva Ram Maganti

Editor
Michael Whalen

Publisher
Sam Van Cook

Publishing Operations Manager
TaneshaNicole Kozler

Publishing Operations Assistant
Charley Eatchel

Social Media and Marketing
Paloma Gomez
Catherine Guden
Eric Tu

OTHER BOOKS BY BUTTON POETRY

If you enjoyed this book, please consider checking out some of our others, below. Readers like you allow us to keep broadcasting and publishing. Thank you!

Kevin Kantor, *Please Come Off-Book*
Ollie Schminkey, *Dead Dad Jokes*
Reagan Myers, *Afterwards*
L.E. Bowman, *What I Learned From the Trees*
Patrick Roche, *A Socially Acceptable Breakdown*
Rachel Wiley, *Revenge Body*
Ebony Stewart, *BloodFresh*
Ebony Stewart, *Home.Girl.Hood.*
Kyle Tran Myhre, *Not A Lot of Reasons to Sing, but Enough*
Steven Willis, *A Peculiar People*
Topaz Winters, *So, Stranger*
Darius Simpson, *Never Catch Me*
Blythe Baird, Sweet, *Young, & Worried*
Siaara Freeman, *Urbanshee*
Robert Wood Lynn, *How to Maintain Eye Contact*
Junious 'Jay' Ward, *Composition*
Usman Hameedi, *Staying Right Here*
Sean Patrick Mulroy, *Hated for the Gods*
Sierra DeMulder, *Ephemera*
Taylor Mali, *Poetry By Chance*
Matt Coonan, *Toy Gun*
Matt Mason, *Rock Stars*
Miya Coleman, *Cottonmouth*
Ty Chapman, *Tartarus*
Lara Coley, *ex traction*
DeShara Suggs-Joe, *If My Flowers Bloom*
Ollie Schminkey, *Where I Dry the Flowers*
Edythe Rodriguez, *We, the Spirits*
Topaz Winters, *Portrait of My Body as a Crime I'm Still Committing*
Zach Goldberg, *I'd Rather Be Destroyed*
Eric Sirota, *The Rent Eats First*
Neil Hilborn, *About Time*
Josh Tvrdy, *Smut Psalm*
Phil SaintDenisSanchez, *before & after our bodies*

Available at buttonpoetry.com/shop and more!

FORTHCOMING BOOKS BY BUTTON POETRY

L.E. Bowman, *Shapeshifter*

Najya Williams, *on a date with disappointment*

Daniel Elias Galicia, *Still Desert*

Hailey M. Tran, *an everyday occurrence*

Chelsea Guevara, *Cipota*

Meg Ford, *Wild/Hurt*

Jared Singer, *Forgotten Necessities*